◈

"Ideally I would like to make a picture
[such] that no two people would see the same thing,
not only because they are different,
but because the picture is different."

Robert Rauschenberg

MISKIN. *Raven Addressing the Assembled Animals.* c.1590. Gouache on paper, 7" x 10½".
Reproduced by Courtesy of the Trustees of the British Museum, London.

COME
LOOK WITH ME

Animals in Art

Gladys S. Blizzard

iːi Charlesbridge

This book is dedicated to my grandchildren—
Julia Blair, Alison, Morgan, and Jack

Published by Charlesbridge
85 Main Street
Watertown, MA 02472
(617) 926-0329
www.charlesbridge.com

Published Under Arrangement with Lickle Publishing, Inc.

Library of Congress Cataloging-in-Publication Data
Blizzard, Gladys S.
    Come look with me: animals in art / Gladys S. Blizzard
        p. cm.
    Summary: Presents twelve color reproductions of paintings of animals
    by such artists as Albrecht Dürer, Paul Klee, and Robert Rauschenberg,
    with questions to stimulate discussion and background information on
    each artist.
        ISBN-13: 978-1-56566-013-7 (reinforced for library use)
        ISBN-10: 1-56566-013-7 (reinforced for library use)
            1. Animals in art—Juvenile literature. 2. Painting—Juvenile
    literature.   [1. Animals in art.   2. Painting.   3. Art appreciation.]
    I. Title II. Title: Animals in art.
    ND1380. B55   1992
    758'.3—dc20   92—5357
                                                                    CIP
                                                                    AC

Production & Design: Charles Davey *design* LLC
Printed in China
(hc) 10 9 8 7 6 5 4 3

Contents

Preface

Animals have been a part of human life and art from the beginning of time. In fact, they were probably the earliest artists' first subjects. The oldest creatures pictured in this book were painted 17,000 years ago, and people have been painting, drawing, and sculpting animals ever since.

As civilization evolves, so do our relationships with animals, and throughout history artists have varied their portrayals accordingly. Sometimes animals represent human traits or are used as symbols, and sometimes they illustrate the wonders of nature. They have always been ideal subjects through which artists could demonstrate their mastery of anatomy and their skill at showing physical action.

The world's art abounds with representations of animals, and it was extremely difficult to narrow the selection for this introductory book to 12 images. One of my aims in doing so was to present a variety of styles which would be encountered again in museums and in books. I hope that this selection will help bring children some new insights about animals, not only as they appear in art, but also as they exist in the natural world.

How to use this book

COME LOOK WITH ME: Animals in Art is part of a series of interactive art appreciation books for young people. Like the other books in the series, this one can be shared with one child or with a small group of children. Each of the 12 paintings is paired with a set of questions meant to stimulate thoughtful discussion between adults and children. The accompanying text, which gives background information on the artist and the painting, can be read silently or aloud by the adult while the children look at the illustrations.

Ask a child to point to part of the painting while he or she discusses it. When working with a group, ask if anyone has a different idea. There are no right or wrong answers to the questions, and everyone will benefit from the different perspectives that experience, age, and personal taste can bring to a group discussion. To keep the interaction lively, it is best to limit each session to the discussion of two or three works of art.

This book can be used in the classroom, at home, and of course, in museums. There is no substitute for a visit to a museum to see the color and texture of an artist's brush strokes and take in the size of an original artwork. However, the methods given here can help children learn a way of looking at original works of art and encourage them to share their understanding with others.

ARTIST UNKNOWN. *Cave Painting.* 15,000 B.C. Lascaux, France. Colorphoto Hans Hinz.

Point to and count all the animals you can find.

Why do you think the artist outlined some and colored others in?

Which animal looks the strongest and most powerful?
How did the artist make it look that way?

Why do you think the artist painted some animals
right over others?

Long, long ago, before people lived in houses or planted crops, animals were humans' main source of food, clothing, and tools. Artists recorded animals' importance by painting them on the walls and ceilings of caves like this one in Lascaux, France.

We can only speculate why the artists produced these paintings of horses, deer, and oxen. They might have painted them to give hunters magical powers over the animals, or out of respect for the great speed and strength the animals possessed.

The colors used in the cave paintings came from minerals in the earth. There is evidence that the minerals were heated and mixed with animal fat to make them stick to the stone walls. The artists probably applied colors with their hands, with brushes made of splintered wood, or by blowing paint through a hollow bone. They sometimes incorporated ridges and bulges in the stone walls into the shoulders or bellies of the animals. By using strong lines and making the most of the few colors they had, they gave a powerful presence to the overlapping group of animals striding across the cave.

MISKIN. *Raven Addressing the Assembled Animals.* c.1590. Gouache on paper, 7" x 10½".
Reproduced by Courtesy of the Trustees of the British Museum, London.

The raven is talking to the animals from a mountaintop.
Point to the animals that don't seem to be paying attention.
Which animals seem to be listening carefully?

Which animals look upset or angry?
Can you find an animal that has a quiet, doubtful look?
How did the artist give the animals their expressions?

The artist made this scene look crowded by cutting some
things off at the edges. Find examples.

In sixteenth-century India, a boy named Akbar inherited the throne at
the age of 14. He introduced many important social reforms and was a
great patron of the arts. Even though he never learned to read or write, he
acquired an impressive library and established a court workshop for
painters who illustrated manuscripts under the guidance of master artists.
The style and subject of the paintings were determined by Akbar, and the
artists' skills and techniques were more important than their originality.

Raven Addressing the Assembled Animals is a manuscript illustration attributed
to Miskin, a master painter during Akbar's reign. Like other Indian artists of
this period, Miskin joined his father in the workshop soon after he could
walk. There he learned to mix paints and make the fine brushes from squirrel
hair that were used to create richly detailed paintings like this one.

This painting illustrates a kind of story called a fable that teaches a les-
son using animals to represent human traits. A black raven perched high
on the mountain looks down upon a gathering of animals and speaks to
them about politics. A phoenix, a fantastic creature with a dragonlike tail,
leads other birds to the assembly. The large group of animals crowds a
landscape of water, land, and sky, and plants and trees cling to the rocky
formation.

ALBRECHT DÜRER. *Saint Eustace.* c. 1500. Engraving.
The National Gallery of Art, Washington, D.C.; Gift of Robert Rosenwald.

Find the castle on the mountain. Do you think it would be easy to get there? Why or why not?

Dürer's engraving is made of many different kinds of lines. Find a dark, heavy line. Find curved lines that make a shape look rounded. How would you compare the horses and deer in this print to the horses and deer in the Lascaux cave painting?

The artist was more interested in showing the animals' anatomy, bones, and muscles, than in portraying them as handsome animals. What can you find in this print that lets you know that?

Albrecht Dürer became an apprentice in his father's goldsmith shop when he was a young boy, as was the custom in Germany in the late 1400s. There he developed great skill using the tools he would later need in the art of printmaking. Though the young artist most wanted to become a painter, he is best known for his detailed prints.

Dürer created *Saint Eustace* with a technique known as engraving. In this process, he used a sharp tool called a burin to cut his design into a metal plate. When his design was complete, he forced ink into the cut lines, wiped away the excess, and pressed the design onto a piece of paper.

In this print, a soldier hunting in the woods kneels in wonder when he sees a crucifix between the antlers of a deer. With thousands of tiny lines, Dürer brings subtle texture, light, and shadow into his composition, portraying the animals, plants, and architecture in realistic detail. In the complex background, closely placed lines in the dark water to the left of the soldier lead our eyes to a white swan and its reflection. A concentration of tiny dots becomes a flock of birds circling the castle tower. A master of anatomy, Dürer demonstrates his ability by showing the five dogs in five different positions. The artist placed his initials at the bottom center of the engraving in a style which became his trademark.

GEORGE STUBBS. *The Grosvenor Hunt.* 1762. Oil on canvas, 59" x 95".
By Kind Permission of His Grace The Duke of Westminster DL.

Which figure seems the most important to you? Why?

Describe or make the sounds that could be heard in this scene.

The dogs are all headed in the same direction, but they are in many different positions. Why do you think the artist painted them that way?

The gray horse and its rider have come to a sudden stop by the river's edge. How has the artist shown us this?

Do you think that this would be a good place to ride a horse? Why or why not?

George Stubbs worked in the family leather business until he was a teenager, when he left to teach himself how to paint. He studied and sketched the anatomy of humans and animals in great detail so that he could paint them as realistically as possible. Though in his lifetime Stubbs was labeled a mere "horse painter," in recent years his work has been recognized for its artistic merits rather than just for its subject matter.

This painting commissioned by Earl Grosvenor, one of the most prosperous men of his day, records an eighteenth-century landowner's sporting activity. The final moments of a hunt are set against a flat landscape and an expansive sky painted in muted tones and with minimal detail. The forceful movement of the hounds splashing into the water is balanced by the oak tree and the huntsman on the gray horse sounding his horn. Earl Grosvenor, wearing a scarlet riding jacket, stops under the arch of the tree, and the huntsmen and their mounts gradually come to a halt near him. Through his carefully planned arrangement of the huntsmen and animals, Stubbs manages to convey the excitement of the hunt without placing too much emphasis on the cornered deer.

EDWARD HICKS. *The Peaceable Kingdom.* ca. 1832–1834. Oil on canvas, 17¼" × 23¼".
Abby Aldrich Rockefeller Folk Art Museum, The Colonial Williamsburg Foundation, Williamsburg, VA.

Name the animals you recognize.

Would you be afraid to walk among these animals? Why or why not?

Find three animal faces turned in profile so that you only see one side of the head. Find two animal faces that appear to be looking straight at you. Find an animal face that shows a three-quarter view so that you see one side and part of the other side.

When Edward Hicks was 13 years old, his father apprenticed him to a coachmaker, from whom he learned the art of decorative painting. As a young man, he became a Quaker minister. He traveled on horseback from one community to another, earning enough to live on by painting signs for streets, shops, and taverns. His style of painting, like that of other artists who were mainly self-taught, is direct and simple, featuring strong outlines and bold, flat colors.

Through his series of "Peaceable Kingdom" paintings, Hicks was able to make a living that was in harmony with the simple life he preached. In the years 1820–1849, he painted many different versions of the biblical prophecy from Isaiah: "the wolf also shall dwell with the lamb, and the leopard shall lie down with the kid and the calf . . . and a little child shall lead them."

An innocent lamb, a patient ox, a proud lion, and other animals symbolizing human qualities are placed in front of a luxurious landscape. The highlights in the clothing, the animal fur, the cloth given to the Indians, the Indians' feathered headdresses, the boat sails, and the clouds in the sky lead our eyes around the painting. At the left, Indians and colonists led by William Penn meet to sign a treaty. In his painting, Hicks expresses his hope for peace both in nature and among men.

What do you think the artist wanted you to notice first about the painting? Why?
What part of the painting is most interesting to you?

How do the horses that are close look different from the ones that are far away?

Does this look like a picture about work or play? Why?

Compare these horses to the horses in *The Grosvenor Hunt*. How are they the same? How are they different?

From an early age, Rosa Bonheur surrounded herself with a wide variety of animals. She made regular visits to slaughterhouses, markets, and the zoo – places where she could study animals and their anatomy, their movements and habits. She believed every creature had a character all its own, and like a portrait painter, she captured the individual traits of each of her subjects.

Bonheur sketched horses and grooms at fairs for months in preparation for this painting. In France in the 1800s, women weren't usually seen in these places. To make sure that she could work without calling attention to herself, she asked the police for permission to dress like a man.

The Horse Fair is dominated by a rhythmic procession of horses and men moving across the canvas toward the slope on the right. Strong blues accent the composition. The vigor and power in the painting are seen in the straining muscles of the horses as they rear, thrash, and prance, as well as in the bulging muscles in their handlers' arms as they try to control them. With powerful arched necks and bowed heads, two gray working horses called Percherons trot side by side, while a nearby pony calmly walks beside its owner. The well-trampled road leads to the fair, where men inspect rows of horses.

ROSA BONHEUR. *The Horse Fair.* 1853–1855. Oil on canvas, 96¼" × 199½".
The Metropolitan Museum of Art. Gift of Cornelius Vanderbilt, 1887 (87.25).
Image © The Metropolitan Museum of Art.

19

MARTIN JOHNSON HEADE. *Cattleya Orchid and Three Brazilian Hummingbirds*. 1871. Oil on wood, 13¾"x 18".
National Gallery of Art, Washington, D.C.; Gift of The Morris and Gwendolyn Cafritz Foundation.

Does this seem like a good place for hummingbirds to have built a nest? Why or why not?

Would you describe the colors in this picture as delicate and subtle, or strong and bold? Why?

Compare the texture of the nest to the texture of the hummingbirds. Compare the texture of the orchid petals to that of the orchid leaves. How do you think the artist made these surfaces appear to have different textures?

The artist has used several methods to balance the images and move our eyes around the entire picture. One method was to repeat the colors in the orchid in other places. Find two places where he has done this.

As a young boy, Martin Johnson Heade was determined to be an artist. His parents arranged for him to take his first lessons from a neighbor, the folk artist Edward Hicks. Later Heade studied in Italy and traveled to the American West and to South America. He started as a portrait painter, then painted landscapes, but he is probably best known for his detailed paintings of orchids and hummingbirds.

These tiny iridescent birds fascinated Heade from boyhood. As an adult, he kept them as pets and trained them to drink sugared water out of his hand. In this composition, as in most of his other paintings, the birds are prominently placed in the foreground, framed by lush vegetation and hanging moss. The transition from the foreground to the vast tropical forest beyond is made through a skillful use of light and atmospheric mist.

Heade composed the exotic landscape based on drawings he made during his trips to South America and visits to hothouses in the United States. He painted from both imagination and memory, thus creating a work with elements of both fantasy and realism.

ARTHUR FITZWILLIAM TAIT. *Rabbits on a Log.* 1897. Oil on canvas, 10" × 12".
The Metropolitan Museum of Art. Gift of Mrs. J. Augustus Barnard, 1979 (1979.490.7).
Image © The Metropolitan Museum of Art.

Where would you have to be to get this view of the rabbits?

Describe how the rabbits' fur would feel if you could touch it.
What are some of the different ways an artist might make it
look this way?

Each of the rabbits is in a different position.
What do you think each one is doing?

Arthur Fitzwilliam Tait grew up on a family farm in England. His
familiarity with animals and his fondness for them would later develop
into the major theme of his art. He was primarily interested in painting
game animals and birds, but it was difficult to find them, since most of
their habitat was privately owned. As a young man he came to America,
where much of the land was open to explore, and pictures of outdoor
sporting scenes were becoming very popular.

For 30 years, Tait sketched and painted scenes in the Adirondack
Mountains. He often ventured alone to sketch from nature, quietly hiding
behind rocks and trees while looking through a telescope to study animals. He even built a large flat bottomed boat which he used as a floating
studio. Tait developed his own technique for painting realistic feathers and
fur; he wrapped corded silk around his finger, then rolled it over the par-
tially dried paint until he achieved the right texture.

The Eastern cottontail rabbits in this painting would have had senti-
mental appeal to people who had moved from farms to the city, reminding
them of what they had left behind. The details in the three rabbits, includ-
ing the highlighting along the edges of their ears and the white sparkle in
their eyes, make the animals stand out against the grass, the daisylike .
flowers, and the pink clover nearby.

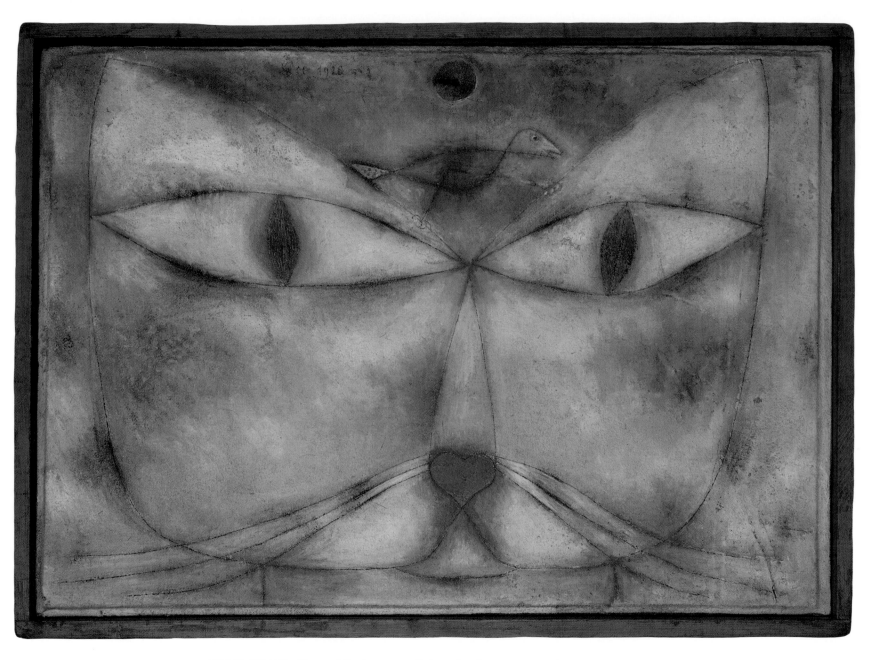

PAUL KLEE. *Cat and Bird*. 1928. Oil and ink on gessoed canvas, 15" × 21".
The Museum of Modern Art, New York. Sidney and Harriet Janis Collection Fund and gift of Suzy Prudden
and Joan H. Meijer in Memory of F. H. Hirschland. © 2008 Artists Rights Society (ARS), New York / VG Bild-Kunst, Bonn.
Digital image © The Museum of Modern Art / Licensed by SCALA / Art Resource, NY.

With your finger, follow the lines the artist used to draw the cat's face. As you do this, look at how the lines change. Describe the changes as you follow them with your finger.

What words would you use to describe the mood of this cat?

Why do you think the artist painted a heart on the cat's nose?

Paul Klee grew up in a home filled with music. He played the violin so well that his parents expected him to become a professional musician. Though music would always be an important part of his life, Klee decided to become an artist.

After years of experimenting with a range of different materials and techniques, Klee's painting style evolved into the creation of fields of color and playful linear images based on his observations of the world around him. In this painting, using just a few lines to form geometric shapes, Klee fills the colorful picture plane with an abstract cat and bird. He was particularly fond of cats and had a number of them at home. In fact, he once said he wished he could be reborn as a cat.

Klee's witty depiction is simple and direct in the way it tells a story. He had a special appreciation of art created by children because of the way young artists express the truth about what they see and know. In *Cat and Bird*, Klee shows us both the outer and inner world of his subject at the same time, something not usually seen in conventional art by adults.

HENRI MATISSE. *The Snail*. 1953. Gouache on paper, 112¾" × 113".
Tate Gallery, London / Art Resource, N.Y.; © 2008 Succession H. Matisse / Artists Rights Society (ARS), New York.

Find the smallest color-shape, put your finger on it, and trace the way the other color-shapes spiral or curl out from that shape.

For this work, the artist cut pieces of painted paper into different shapes and pasted them on white paper. Point to several places where you can see brush marks.

Which color touches every other color?

This picture is called *The Snail*.
Why do you think the artist called it that?

When Henri Matisse was recovering from an illness at the age of 20, his mother gave him some brushes and paints to help him pass the time. From then on his interest in art grew. When he told his parents he wanted to leave the law profession to become an artist, his father warned him that he would die of hunger. In time, however, Matisse became a well-respected and successful artist noted for his masterful use of color and all its expressive qualities.

After years of painting vivid canvases and filling the space with images in strong, colored patterns, Matisse began to experiment with paper cutouts like *The Snail*. He directed his assistants to paint sheets of paper in the colors he chose, then he cut shapes out of them, placing the cutouts on a background to emphasize color relationships.

For this work, Matisse studied real snails, drawing and redrawing them until he was able to express the essence of their form. What looks simple and spontaneous resulted from careful observation of his subject and a thoughtful representation of its rhythm and shape, rather than an attempt to copy it in nature. Matisse often remarked that it took a lot of experience to enable him to create something so simple.

ROY DEFOREST. *Canoe of Fate.* 1974. Acrylic on canvas, 66¾" × 90¼".
Philadelphia Museum of Art. Purchased with the Adele Haas Turner and Beatrice Pastorius Turner Memorial Fund.

Find four different ways the artist painted eyes.

Find an animal that looks real. Then find an animal that looks much less real. Compare the two and discuss what it is about them that made you make your decisions.

Would you say this is a quiet and serious painting or a lively and humorous one? Why?

Would you like to be a passenger in the canoe?
Why or why not?

As a boy, Roy DeForest liked to read adventure stories about explorers and naturalists. Today, many of his paintings portray journeys in which animals and people find their way together.

Within his work, DeForest creates a richly imaginative world full of patterns, bright colors, and unusual characters. In *Canoe of Fate*, a woman, an Indian, and several animals travel by canoe through a crazy-quilt landscape. The animals and humans seem equals in steering their passage through a magical place. Their eyes are wide and staring, looking inward as much as outward.

In this painting, as in many of his others, DeForest's intense colors, varied textures, and wacky characters resemble those in comic strips, and the scene is full of wit and humor. In *Canoe of Fate*, DeForest paints a haunting world that seems to tell a story, though we can only tell our own version because the haunting images are from the artist's own fantasy.

ROBERT RAUSCHENBERG. *Wall-Eyed Carp/ROCI Japan.* 1987. Acrylic-and-fabric collage on canvas, 80″ x 243″.
National Gallery of Art, Washington, D.C.; Gift of the Robert Rauschenberg Foundation.
© Robert Rauschenberg /VAGA, New York 1992.

When a group of lines is repeated, a pattern results. Point to the places where lines make a pattern.

Can you find some of the places where it looks as if the artist splashed paint? Why do you think the artist used paint this way?

In this work of art, the artist included objects from a trip he took to Japan: a kite, a map of the country, and photographs. He wanted to share with us some of his impressions and challenge us to find our own meaning in them. What does this collage tell you about Japan and about the artist?

Robert Rauschenberg constantly experiments with materials, combining painting with real objects he finds. When we look at his work, we see new ways of making art. He encourages us to think about the creative process and to look closely at the everyday objects around us.

He credits his mother with the beginning of his interest in collage, a kind of composition in which objects are glued to a surface and organized with added lines and color. When he was growing up during the Depression, his mother cut patterns from fabric so carefully that no material was wasted.

This collage was made for an international exhibition Rauschenberg organized to promote world peace and understanding. For this exhibit, he traveled to 10 countries in six years, taking photographs, collecting objects, and meeting with artists and writers.

For *Wall-Eyed Carp*, Rauschenberg glued a large kite, fabric, and a map of Japan onto his canvas. Some of the artist's photographs of people in Japan were transferred to the canvas by a silkscreen printing process. The fish is a carp, which traditionally symbolizes perseverance and courage. In Japan each May, fish kites like this one are flown on tall poles to celebrate Children's Day.

Look at all the pictures again.

Which animals seem most comfortable in the landscape?

Which animals do you think were most difficult to draw? Why?

Which animals would you like as pets?

Which picture is your favorite?

If you keep looking, you'll notice different things, and will probably have new ideas each time you look.